The First Christmas Gift

By Trecia Watson

The First Christmas Gift

by

Trecia Watson

This labor of love is dedicated to Shannon, Trecia Watson's daughter.

Illustrated by Trecia Watson

COPYRIGHT 2007-Trecia Watson

God created the Heavens and earth. God created animals and man. God placed man in the Garden of Eden. God told man to not eat fruit on one tree. Man disobeyed.

Man had sinned by eating of the apple. God was displeased with man and woman. He ordered Adam and Eve to leave the beautiful garden that He had created. No longer would Adam and Eve be allowed to enjoy the wonderful garden that God had created for man. Adam and Eve left the garden to enter the world beyond.

God does not like sin. Disobeying God is sin. God could not look at man and woman after they disobeyed Him. God could see their sin. God had an idea. He would send His own Son to earth as Savior.

Jesus would come to earth as a baby. He would live upon this earth as human. Jesus would grow up into a man. Jesus would please God.

Man would watch Jesus as He lived as man. Man would learn how to please God.

Jesus would be attacked by evil men. Jesus would be accused of doing bad thing. He would be beaten by these evil men and hung on a cross to die. Jesus' body would be put in a borrowed tomb. But Jesus would not stay. He would rise on the third day.

Jesus would save His people from their sins. If man sinned, man could ask God to forgive him. God would forgive man for his sins if man accepted Jesus. Jesus was this wonderful gift that God would give to man. God gave His only begotten son to man as the first Christmas gift.

God chose a very kind woman to be Jesus' mother. Her name was Mary. Mary was to marry Joseph. When Joseph found out that Mary was going to have a baby, Joseph was worried. An angel came to Joseph as he slept and told Joseph to not be afraid. The angel told Joseph that God had sent the baby and was pleased. This baby was God's son.

So Joseph took Mary as His wife. Mary and Joseph would be the earthly parents of Jesus. Jesus was God's son sent to earth to help man. Jesus would save His people from their sins. Mary and Joseph waited for Jesus to be born.

In the land of Judea in the city of David a donkey was born. This little donkey's name was Earl.

Earl was unlike other donkeys. God had made Earl with a special tail and ears. God had work for Earl to do. That is how God does things. He first has a plan. Then everything happens to follow that plan.

God made Earl's ears very long and furry. God made Earl's tail very long and strong. Earl's ears and tail did not look like the ears and tails of other donkeys. All the other donkeys and children laughed at little Earl. Earl was a sad little donkey.

Earl did not know about God and God's plan. One day Earl had decided to run away from his home. He got dressed in his 'run-away-from-home cloths' and began his journey. Earl began to cry.

Then an angel came and spoke to Earl. "Special little donkey," the angel called. "Don't run away. Please stop crying. You were made by a loving God. You were made like God wanted you made. God has a special work for you to do."

Earl stopped in his tracks. Earl also dried up his 'fill sorry for me' tears with his long furry ears. Earl asked the angel, "Why do my donkey friends and the children laugh and call me names?"

The angel said, "Your donkey friends and the children don't understand. They are not looking at everything as God sees everything. God has a divine purpose in everything He does. God does not make mistakes. You will understand one day."

The angel faded into the night. Earl waited for the moment when God would need his ears and tails.

The special night for all the world was about to come to pass. Mary and Joseph had to go to Bethlehem on important business. The night was filled with angry winds. The winds stirred up the sand. The roads to Bethlehem were nearly empty of travelers. No one could see for the wind was blowing sand over hills, through the valleys and over roads.

Mary and Joseph worried about traveling to Bethlehem. Mary was going to have a baby very soon and she could not walk. The couple had no donkey for Mary to ride. And the wind storm was so bad that Joseph could not see. What were they to do?

The angel of the Lord came to Earl. The angel told Earl that God needed him this night. The angel told Earl that he was to carry Mary and lead Joseph through the sand storm to Bethlehem. Earl was so pleased that he was a part of God's special plan.

Earl came to Joseph. When Joseph saw Earl, the special little donkey, Joseph knew God had sent Earl.

Earl kneeled down on the ground. Mary climbed on Earl's back. Earl carried Mary to Bethlehem. The sand was blowing very hard and thick. Earl wrapped Mary with his long furry ears. Earl led Joseph through the night with his long strong tail.

A special note just for you……….

So dear child, remember these words. ***"God knows what He is doing. He made you so very special. You are not like anyone else in the world. God made you for a special job too."***

Sometimes there will be others who will not understand about you. People who don't follow God don't understand about everything. People make fun of things they don't understand. People should be ashamed of themselves. People pick on others who are smaller, and weaker. God sees these people do these mean things. God does not like this. God will teach these people a lesson one day. Remember, God is the one in control, and God has a plan for you.

A bright star was shinning over Bethlehem. The star had appeared many nights ago. It was getting brighter and brighter each night. Men and women throughout the world had heard about the bright star. The star shined from heaven pointing the way to Jesus' birth.

The story of God sending His son as Savior had spread through the ages. Now this wondrous star was pointing the way to Bethlehem. Many who had heard the story of Jesus' birth followed the star. Shepherds watching their sheep at night wondered about the star. Many shepherds left their sheep alone to follow the star to a stable in Bethlehem.

A little shepherd boy named Ken cared for his sheep. Ken wondered about the bright star. The star was calling, but Ken could not leave his sheep.

An angel came and said, "Come. You shall find the babe wrapped in swaddling clothes, lying in a manger." Ken followed the star to the stable.

You know about the Christmas tree. You know about Santa and presents. These wonderful things make Christmas very special. For truly, Jesus' birthday is the most special time of the year.

This night was a very wonderful night. The son of God was born. Jesus was born in Bethlehem in a stable. Jesus was laid in a manger, because there was no room for Him in the inn.

All creatures, large and small, came to see this thing which had happened in Bethlehem. Near the stable grew a large tree. All fowl and climbing creatures made their way to this tree. Each found a limb on which to perch. Each watched as shepherds and wise men gathered around the stable.

The light from the star lit up the valley around the stable. The light shinned upon the tree. The eyes of the creatures in the tree shinned as lights.

Angels throughout the world and heaven had gathered around Bethlehem. They too wanted to witness the special events that were occurring. Angels also came to sing praises to Jesus. Angel voices filled the night sky, saying "Glory to God in the highest, and on earth, Peace, Good Will toward men."

A young angel named Shannon came to the stable with the other angels. Shannon's wings were not yet large enough to hold her up. She could fly, but she could float in one place.

Shannon also had a tiny voice. Her singing could not be heard above the singing voices of the older angels. Shannon began to sigh. She wanted to be a part of this special night also.

The charge angel approached Shannon. "Why are you crying my dear," asked the charge angel?"

"I want to do something for Baby Jesus too," Shannon said.

The charge angel spoke, "You can sing with the other angels."

"No one can hear me. My voice is too soft," Shannon cried.

The charge angel thought for a moment. He looked around the stable. He looked at the large tree filled with shinning eyes. The charge angel had a wonderful idea.

"You can climb up the world's first Christmas tree and sit on top. You will look beautiful sitting on the top. You will make the world's first Christmas tree so very special," the charge angel explained.

Shannon loved that idea. Shannon ran to the trunk of the tree and began climbing through the limbs. Each creature who sat in the tree helped Shannon as she climbed through the limbs.

Shannon finally reached the top. She positioned herself in the top of the world's first Christmas tree. She stretched out her wings and sang soft praises to baby Jesus, the world's first Christmas gift.

In a nearby country three camels were born. This was a most unusual site. All the children from near and far came to see the camels.

The camels were named Anna, Hanna, and Santa. Santa played with the children. He would rather play with the children than with his own brother camels. The children loved Santa also.

The story about Jesus spread throughout the world. Wise men heard about Jesus and searched for the young child. The wise men followed the star. The wise men traveled a long way, bringing gifts for the baby. The three camels also carried gifts for Jesus. Anna carried hay for his bed, Hanna carried water, and Santa carried toys and special treats.

Children followed behind the three camels. Santa played with the children and sang special songs. Santa gave out toys and treats to the children. All the children were fully dressed in their 'laugh till we cry' play clothes. Santa had never had so much fun. Santa wished that he could be human. He wished he could keep giving out toys and treats to children.

The journey to Bethlehem took the wise men and camels over many high hills and through many low valleys. As the journey continued, Santa had no more gifts in his big red bag. He had given out all the toys and treats to the children. Before night time came, the children returned to their homes.

Santa was sad. The children were no longer following the camels. Santa was also sad because he had given away all the toys and treats that were supposed to be given to baby Jesus.

When the caravan arrived at the stable, the wise men presented their gifts of gold, frankincense, and mirth. Then the camels gave their gifts to Jesus. Anna presented baby Jesus with bags of new straw for His manger. Hanna presented baby Jesus with fresh clean water. When Santa's turn came, Santa had no more gifts in his packs. He had given out all his toys and treats to the children. Santa wept.

God was watching from Heaven as people throughout Bethlehem gathered for the birth of Jesus. God was excited about seeing Jesus too. God saw all creatures surrounding the stable. God saw the shepherds. God saw the wise men and camels.

God also saw deep in Santa's heart. God granted Santa's wish. God turned Santa into a human so he could give toys on Christmas to boys and girls throughout the world.

Santa was so very happy. He was now standing on two feet instead of four. He could also give hugs with his arms. Santa rejoiced in a very strange way. He crabbed his big belly with his hands. His happy sound of "Ho, Ho, Ho" filled the air.

Baby Jesus was visited by many people on this mystical night. Many brought gifts. Because the stable was so very small, the visitors left their gifts under the large tree near the stable. This was truly the world's first Christmas tree.

God was pleased at what He saw. His wondrous plan of salvation had come to earth. Jesus came to earth to save His people from their sins. Now people all over the world could accept Jesus as their savior. People would be happier, and so would God.

For God so loved the world that He gave His Only Begotten Son that whosoever believeth on Him should not perish, but have eternal life.

For God send not His Son into the world to condemn the world, but that the world through Him might be saved. Whosoever believeth upon the Only Begotten Son of God shall be saved.

Jesus grew up and did what God wanted Him to do. He taught people how to live good lives. He healed sick people. He raised people from the dead. This made religious leaders mad. These leaders did not want Jesus doing these things. These leaders were evil.

As time went on, more people believed as the evil leaders believed. Jesus was finally captured by these evil people. Jesus was nailed to an old rugged cross.

Jesus died on the cross between two thieves. He gave His life so that we could have eternal life.

Jesus' body was laid in a tomb. A tomb is a large cave for burial. The soldiers rolled a large stone over the tomb. On the third day, Jesus rose from the dead.

This is why we celebrate Easter. On Good Friday Jesus died after being nailed to the cross. Jesus was in the tomb for three days, and on Sunday, Jesus rose from the dead.

All of nature celebrates Jesus rising from the dead. In the spring all flowers, grass, and trees spring forth with new life. Little chicks are born, and baby ducks. Baby rabbits come from their burrows. All of nature comes alive in the spring, as Jesus came alive from the tomb.

Eggs are a sign of new life. We decorate eggs with pretty colors. Though we can't create new life as God can create new life, we can decorate eggs, as a symbol of new life. Then the eggs are hidden from sight the way Jesus was hidden from sight by being buried in the tomb. We look for the eggs as people throughout the ages looked for Jesus. Many followed the star. Men still seek Jesus and ask Jesus to come into their hearts.

The child who finds the most eggs, or the largest egg, is awarded a prize. Likewise, the person who finds Jesus will be awarded a prize. We will have peace for this life. We will also be awarded eternal life. Easter is a symbol of new life.

Some people get caught up in coloring eggs, and buying Easter baskets. Some people don't know about Jesus. The Easter eggs, baskets, rabbits, chicks, and ducks are extra things about Easter. Jesus dying on the cross and arising from the dead are the most important.

Jesus is watching after those who believe in Him. He hears us when we pray. He answers our prayers. He cares for us the way a shepherd cares for his sheep.

If you will ask God to forgive you for your sins and believe that Jesus is the Son of God, Jesus will save you today. Then you will be able to walk with God throughout each day. God will hear your prayers. God will help you as you go throughout each day. One day you will be able to go to Heaven to be with Jesus.

If you will say the following prayer and believe, Jesus will save you today.

"Dear God, please forgive me, for I am a sinner. I believe in Jesus and I accept Jesus as my savior. I believe Jesus was born as a baby and was nailed to a cross for my sins. Come into my heart today. Amen."

When Jesus comes into your heart your heart feels lighter and happier. You now have a Heavenly Father who will talk to your heart and help you.

You may be wondering how God talks to us. God talks to us through the Bible. The Bible is God's words to man. The Bible tells us what to do. The Bible tells us what not to do. When Jesus comes in our hearts, the Holy Spirit of God will lead us to do right things. The Holy Spirit will whisper to our hearts. God will talk to us through the Holy Spirit.

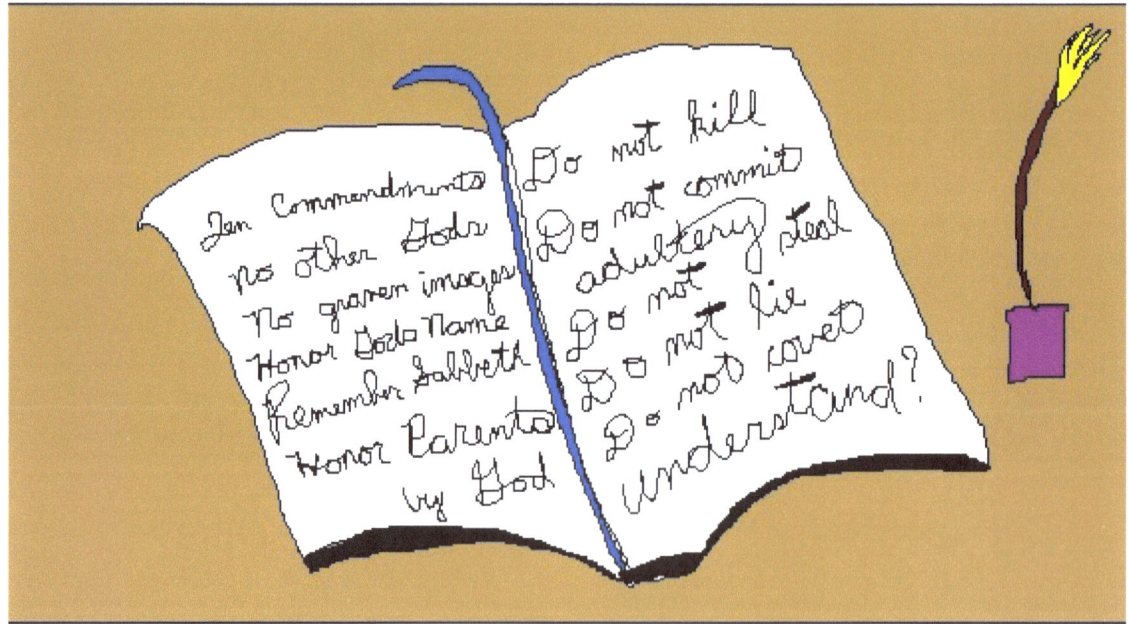

We won't listen to evil voices. We will only listen to God. And when we sin, we are sorry for our sins. We ask God to forgive us. If we keep doing the same thing over and over, we were not sorry for what we did the first time. God knows that.

After you accept Jesus as Savior, you must follow God's commandments. You must please God, and do what the Bible tells you to do.

Accepting Jesus as your savior is more than believing in Jesus. Even the devil believes in Jesus. Accepting Jesus as your savior is more than going to church. Even the devil goes to church. When we accept Jesus as savior we do what the Bible says to do. When we accept Jesus as our savior we pray and ask God to lead us. When God tells us to do something, we do it. When God tells us not to do something, we don't do it.

When we sin, we tell God we are sorry. We ask God to forgive us for our sins. God will not forgive us unless we are sorry for what we have done. People who keep doing bad things over and over are not sorry for what they do. People who keep doing the same evil things are not saved.

People who are saved will make mistakes. If we do something wrong one time that may be a mistake. If we do the same thing wrong two times, that may be a mistake. But if we do something over, and over, and over, we are not making mistakes. We are listening to evil voices within us.

A Christian will not listen to evil voices over and over and over. A Christian will say, "No," to evil voices. God will help us to say, "No!" to evil voices. This is what the Bible says. The Bible is only truth.

What a wonderful gift God gave to the world on that first Christmas. Jesus is the reason we have

Christmas. Evil people of the world try to take Christ out of Christmas. Evil people nailed Jesus to a cross. But evil people cannot take Christ out of our hearts. Christ is alive in the hearts of Christian people.

God lives in your heart too, if you prayed the prayer above and accept Jesus as your savior. The blood that Jesus shed on the cross covers your sins. And Jesus will lead you and help you not to sin again. And if you do sin, you can ask Jesus to forgive you, and Jesus will.

What a wonderful time when this life is over and you live in Heaven with Jesus. You will meet all your loved ones who are already in Heaven. You will see your grand-parents, and other family members. We will live for eternity in heaven.

Those who do not know Jesus as Savior will not go to heaven. There is another place for people who do not believe. It is not a good place. People who go to this place will not be happy. They will suffer pain and agony. These people will live with devils and evil people. It will not be a happy time for them. These people will never see their families again. These people will never see God or heaven.

God wants us to tell others about Jesus. We must get people to listen to us. God doesn't want anyone to miss heaven. God loves everyone. God loves people who do evil. He loves people who laugh at others, like the children who laughed at Earl.

Often people do things that God does not like. The children laughed at Earl, the special little donkey. These children were listening to hateful voices within them. These children did not know Earl. They only laughed because Earl was different. People are afraid of others who are different. When people are afraid they make fun of others. People throw off on others when they don't feel good about themselves.

People often don't listen to God's loving voice. Sometimes men and women steal, and lie. Sometimes people tell lies on others. God does not want us to laugh at others, or hurt others in anyway. God wants us to love others. God wants us to do good things. God wants us to obey our parents.

God loves people who don't follow the Ten Commandments. God wants these people to be saved.

People who make fun of others need to be saved. People who do the same bad things, over and over, need to be saved. People who lie, and cheat, and manipulate others need to be saved. People who steal, and kill and cause others to cry need to be saved.

God wants everyone to be saved. God wants Christians to tell everyone about Jesus. .

If you believe and asked God to save you, you are now a Christian. Now you can tell people about Jesus. Jesus is God's Christmas gift to the world.

The End

About the Author

When I was a child, I lived next door to my grand-parents, my mother's mom and dad. When I got old enough to sit still for a while, Mammaw Taylor took me to church with her. There were a lot of Sundays that I was anything but still, but Mammaw Taylor continued to take me to church with her.

One day the preacher asked those who wanted to be saved to come forward for prayer. I went up and was saved. I was nine years old at the time. I was never the same from that day forward. I learned the Lord's Prayer and recited it every day, praying to God. When things started going wrong for me, when I felt myself faced with problems, I prayed. When someone hurt my feelings, I prayed. Prayer became a big part of my life as a child.

As I grew in the Lord, I leaned on Him even more. I could not have gone through one day without prayer and talking to the Lord. I prayed about all my challenges.

I played sports in school: basketball. I was a forward. Every time I aimed to take a shot at the basket, I always prayed, "Let this one go in," and s-w-i-s-h, the ball went in, hitting nothing but the inside of the net. Jesus helped me do what I did on the basketball court. I was a well known basketball star, always listed on the All District and All Region Tournament teams. Once I made All-State. I was on every All-Tournament team that existed when I played basketball, from fifth grade to my senior year. More often than not, I was the Most Valuable Player during each tournament. I was asked to play basketball for a renown ladies basketball team ... The Red Heads.

As I became older, I saw God working in my life more and more. I witnessed miracles. When I prayed about a horrible situation, I saw God work in mighty ways. I was convinced that God was near me and was listening to my prayers. Therefore, I tried to always do what was right, and never do anything to hurt someone else or God. I believed that God was watching everything that happened, and I didn't want God to turn His head from me when I prayed. Often people think, *no one is watching*, and they do want they want to do, regardless. How sad when they find out ... God is watching and recording everything that occurs!

I often sat in church listening to visiting speakers share horrible stories of being involved in alcohol and drugs, and other things some people do. These speakers told about turning to God and how God made a difference for them. Everyone listening seemed to be intrigued about the speakers leaving a life of sin and coming to God. I was never intrigued but glad that these people did find God. I had always walked with God and was thankful I had not gotten mixed up in sin at any time through my life.

God cares for you as much as He cares for me. While you are young, before you get mixed up in sin that the devil throws out in front of you, give your life to Jesus. He will never fail you, but will be there for you, as He has been and *is* there for me. Amen!

by

Trecia Watson

www.ingramcontent.com/pod-product-compliance
Lightning Source LLC
Chambersburg PA
CBHW042133070426
42453CB00002BA/74